This book belongs
to
....

ENJOY

This book contains balnk pages left intentionally to assist with removal framing or display and minimize bleed through. HOWEVER, feel free to use it the way you like.

TRICK
OR
TREAT

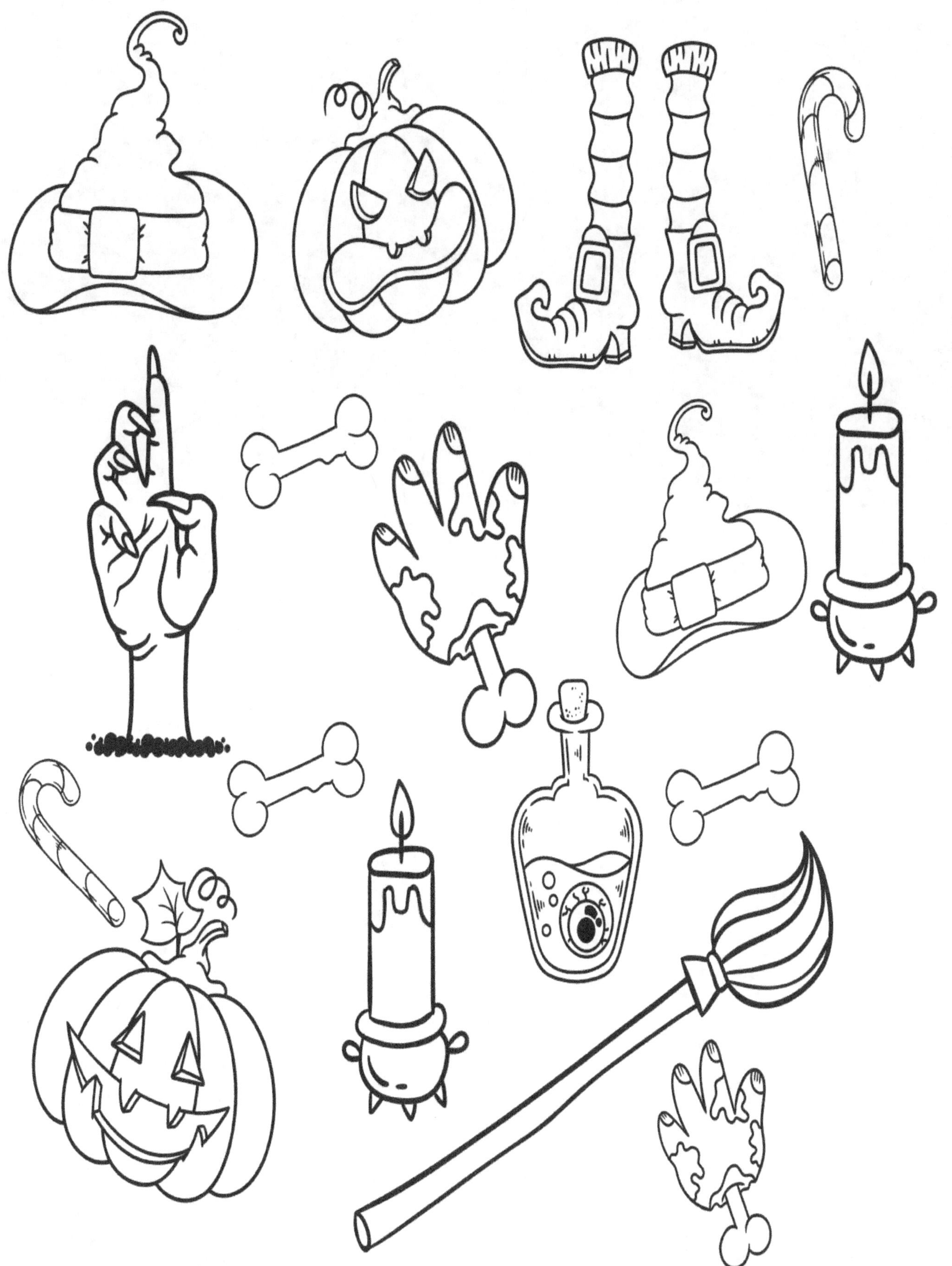

BOO!
RIP
RIP
RIP

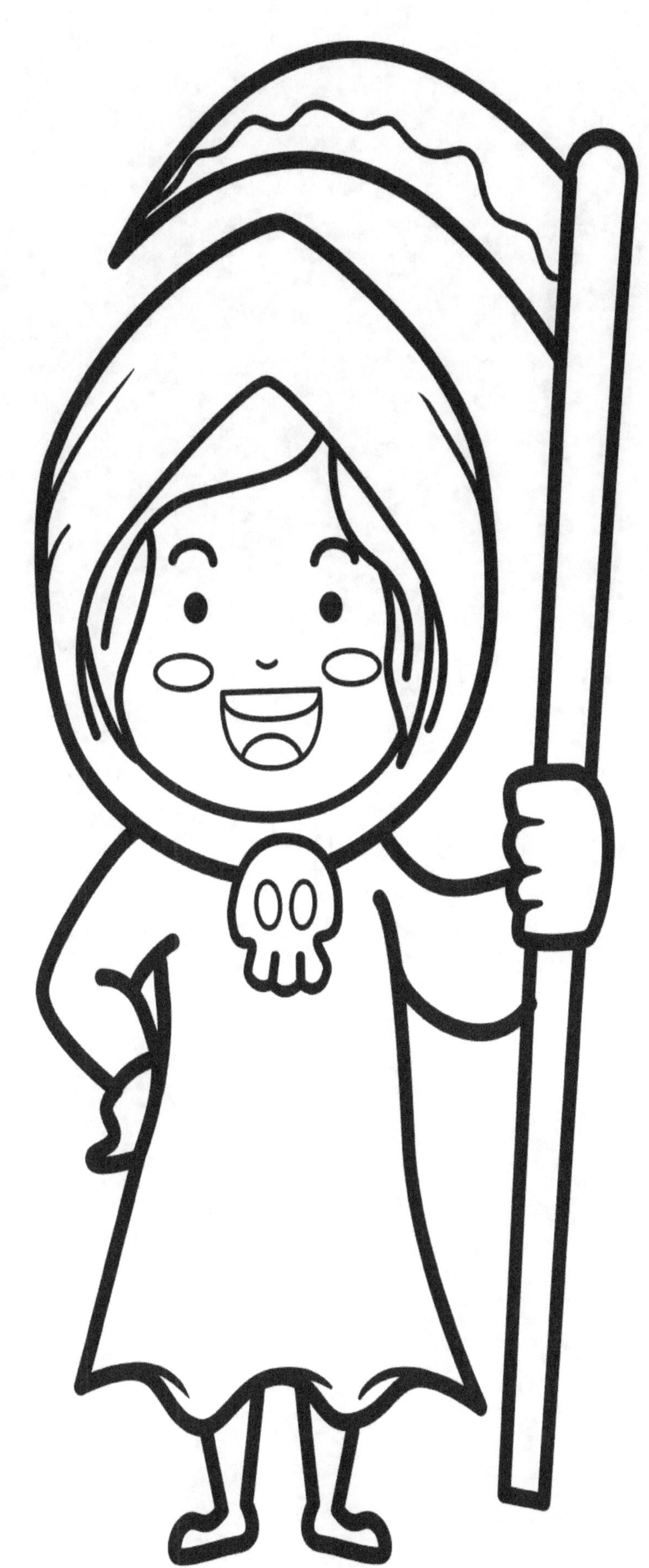

TRICK
OR
TREAT

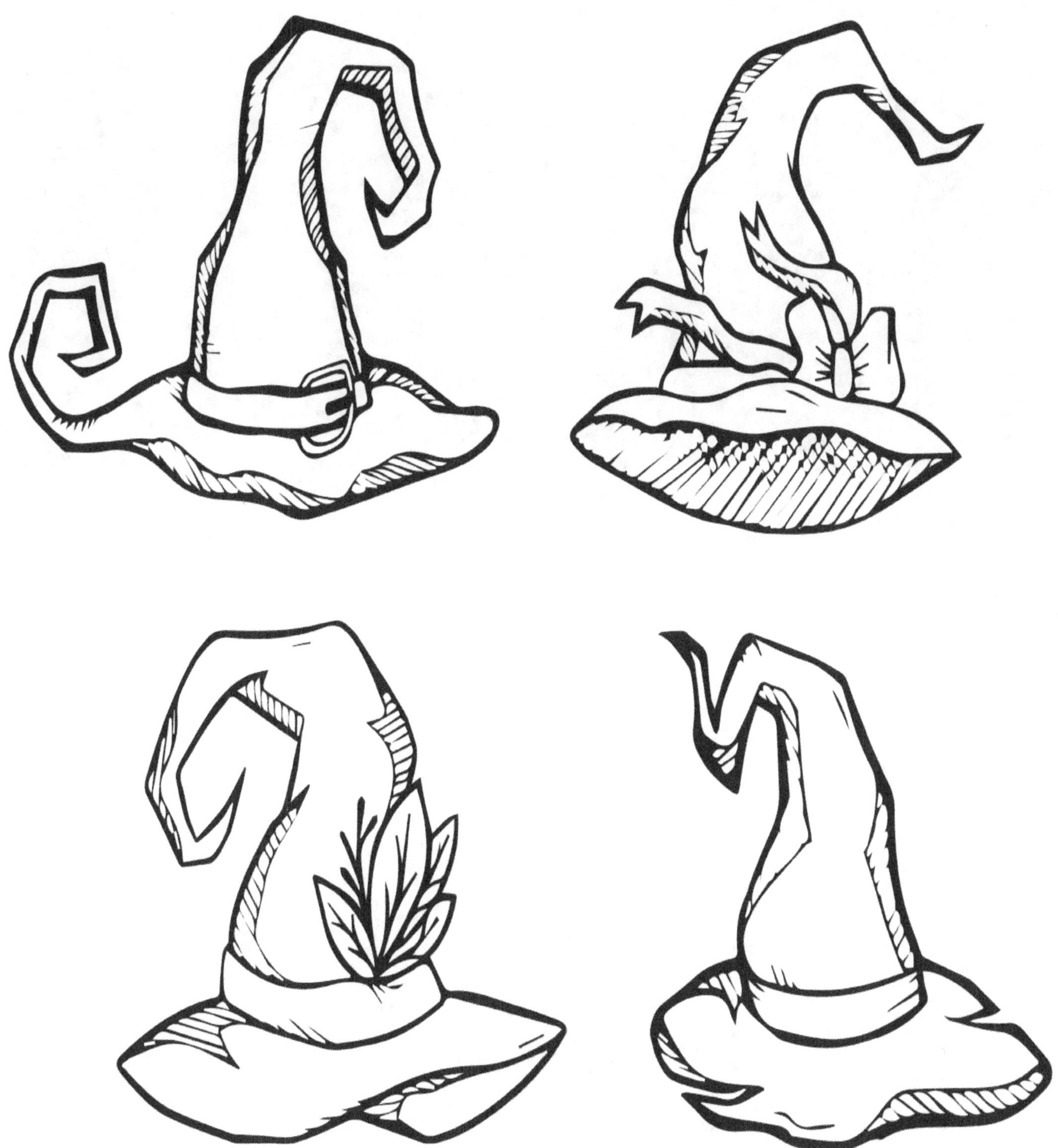

EYE
of
NEWT